George Patton Jr.

George S. Patton Jr. and Andrew "Nuts" McAuliffe. Source: U.S. Army

NOTES ON BASTOGNE OPERATION

DALE STREET BOOKS
Silver Spring, Maryland

The relief of Bastogne is the most brilliant operation we have thus far performed and is in my opinion the outstanding achievement of this war. Now the enemy must dance to our tune, not we to his.
– George S. Patton Jr.

Paratroopers of the 101st Airborne moving up to Bastogne. Source: U.S. Army

Annotations and Introduction
by Aleksandra M. Rohde

TABLE OF CONTENTS

INTRODUCTION

Bold Plans

On September 16, 1944 Hitler convened a "special meeting with a small circle," among them General Alfred Jodl, who had been slightly injured in the attempt on Hitler's life the previous July, General Heinz Guderian, Chief of the General Staff of the German Army and General Werner Kreipe, Chief of Staff for the German Air Force. Jodl began briefing the sober statistics on comparative strength between Allied and Wehrmacht forces. The Allies had already deployed into theatre 96 divisions with 10 more divisions on the way. The Germans could muster only 55 divisions. And those divisions were sorely in need of equipment and supplies. "Parachute and airborne troops [were] still at their garrisons. [There was a] lack of heavy weapons, ammunition and panzers."[i]

The Fuehrer interrupted Jodl. Despite the seemingly bad news, Hitler had an audacious plan. Rather than follow his staff's advice to allow the depleted units time to rest and rehabilitate, Hitler instead ordered a counterattack from the Ardennes. The objective was the Belgium port city of Antwerp, a vital gateway for Allied supplies pouring into the European theatre. The following is from General Kreipe's diary entry for September 14:

> [Hitler reasoned that] forces [were] equal because of the positions and the strength of the defense. [He stated that] the present front [could] be held easily! Our attack group [would consist of] 30 new Volksgrenadier divisions and new panzer divisions in addition to panzer divisions from

the East. [This would be an] attempt to bust the seam between the British and the Americans, [it would be the] new Dunkirk." Guderian protested because of the [precarious] situation in the East. Jodl point[ed] to the [Allied] superiority in the air and expectation of parachute landings in Holland, Denmark and Northern Germany. Hitler requested 1500 fighter planes by 1 Nov! My suggestion to stop immediately the commitment of the fighter planes from the rehabilitation groups and my pointing to the lack of airfields there, is being rejected. Pointed remarks. Offensive should be launched during the bad weather period, then the enemy cannot fly either. [Gerd von] Rundstedt is to take over the command. Preparations up to 1 Nov. the Fuehrer again summarizes his decision in a long discourse. Binds us by obligation to maintain strict secrecy and asks us to employ few and reliable men. Afterwards brief discussion with Jodl relative to the new situation; have still to think it over myself. Briefed Goering who flies back to Carinhall at night. Return to Rosengarten. I am quite tired, headache."[ii]

The Allies had landed on the beaches of Normandy two months before and were now charging east toward Germany. In the east, the Soviets were camped at the edge of Warsaw, waiting to capture the city on their drive west toward Berlin. In the German homeland, the relentless Allied bombing of factories, railway lines, bridges and even civilian targets, was rattling the nerves of Hitler's once resolute nation and steadily degrading its capability to wage war.

Hitler was cornered and desperately needed a bold plan to stall the advancing Allies; buy the time needed to replenish forces worn out by fighting on two fronts,[iii] field the modern weapons still in development,[iv] boost morale of the German populace, and perhaps negotiate a more favorable peace treaty. He just needed the right conditions.

The weather that occurs in the Ardennes and Eifel terrain during the winter generally is severe, and it was in 1944. This is mountainous country, with much rainfall, deep snows in winter, and raw, harsh winds sweeping across the plateaus. The heaviest rains occur in November and December. The mists are frequent and heavy, lasting well into late morning before they break...freezing weather [at Bastogne] averages 145 days. The structure of the soil will permit tank movement when the ground is frozen, but turns into a clayey mire in time of rain. A single snow storm often deposits a depth of 10 to 12 inches in a 24-hour period.[v]

Predictably, heavy rains in early December 1944, followed soon after by blustery snows, transformed once traversable Ardennes roads into rivulets of slippery mud. The low-hanging storm clouds created a thick grey soup making it difficult to see down the road, let alone while flying through the skies. Faced with treacherous travel conditions, the Allies hunkered down waiting for the storms to pass. The weather was indeed awful but to the Germans it provided a strategic advantage.[vi] In the near-zero visibility, German forces could shield their movements and conceal their positions — a stroke of good luck for what they were about to undertake.[vii]

Hitler arrived on the Western Front to personally supervise the operation. On December 12th he called his division commanders to a secret meeting in a village near Field Marshal Gerd von Rundstedt's headquarters.

The division commanders first were assembled at Von Rundstedt's CP. There SS guard stripped them of their side arms and pocket knives. They then were loaded into busses and driven around the countryside for a half-hour, with SS guards trailing each bus. The column finally halted before a building and the generals were led into a room where they found Hitler, flanked by Field Marshal Keitel and Colonel General Jodl. Hitler delivered a two-hour briefing on the details of the offensive. He announced Antwerp as the major objective, and sternly ordered that it be captured in fourteen days. No one else did any talking. Occasionally, Keitel and Jodl nodded their heads in approval. But Hitler did all the speaking. Throughout the meeting, SS guards, with burp guns at the read, maintained a cold-eyed scrutiny of the generals.[viii]

The episode was relayed months later to an Allied interrogator by captured Major General Hans Waldenburg, commanding general of the 116th Panzer Division.

It was an uncomfortable feeling...sitting there with all those guards watching every move we made. There we sat, receiving orders from der Fuehrer for a major campaign and at the same time not daring to reach into the pocket for a handkerchief. Der Fuehrer looked ill but he spoke with fire and spiritual frenzy.[ix]

That preparations for the German offensive caught the Allies by complete surprise was due to German stealth and tactical ingenuity. Captured documents detailing preparations for the offensive, indicated the Germans utilized 1,050 trains to move men and equipment into position in complete secrecy and without any interruption of regularly scheduled train travel.[x]

But the successful surprise attack was also due in part to the belief by some of the Allies' leadership — most notably the British under Field Marshal Bernard Montgomery — who were convinced the German forces were irreversibly depleted and therefore would not attack. On December 12, just four days before the Germans launched their offensive, the British Weekly Intelligence Summary, stated, "It is now certain that attrition is steadily sapping the strength of German forces on the Western Front and the crust of defense is thinner, more brittle, and more vulnerable..."[xi]

In the blustery early morning of December 16, the Germans launched their Hail Mary offensive with blistering artillery fire from the east through the thick Ardennes forest. German tanks and men advanced quickly against the stunned Allies. American forces were taking the brunt of the fighting in the First Army sector of the Western Front.

At the time Patton's Third Army area of operations was south of First Army and preparing to move east toward the Siegfried line.[xii] However, by December 12, Patton had become alarmed enough by the reports of increasing German movements and growing strength along the east side of the First Army front that he asked his staff (Chief of Staff Hobart R. Gay and Halley G. Maddox, Operations Chief) to prepare plans for what Third Army would do in the event of a "break-through."[xiii]

General Dwight D. Eisenhower, the Supreme Allied Commander in Europe, assembled his senior Allied commanders on December 19 near Verdun for an emergency meeting. Among the group assembled was General George S. Patton Jr., Commander of Third Army, whom Eisenhower respected but who he also knew could be impulsive and outspoken at times. He once had counseled Patton to "count to ten before you speak."[xiv] But Patton was also indispensable, having proven himself to be one of the war's finest battlefield commanders, with a string of victories in North Africa, Sicily and now decisively roaring toward Germany.

Eisenhower was newly promoted to his fifth star. He received his fourth star just before the heavy American casualties suffered at Kasserine Pass in 1943. He joked to Patton, "Funny thing, George, every time I get another star, I get attacked." Patton responded, "Every time you get attacked, Ike, I have to bail you out."[xv] At the meeting in Verdun Eisenhower asked Patton how long it would take to turn the Third Army north to assist the First. Patton said, "Days hell, we are already on the way!"[xvi] Patton came prepared with a plan his staff had already formulated to stop the German advance.

Patton's proposal was astonishing, technically difficult, and daring. It meant reorienting his entire Army from an eastward direction to the north, a 90-degree turn that would pose logistical nightmares — getting divisions on new roads and making sure that supplies reached them from dumps established in quite a different context, for quite a different situation. Altogether, it was an operation that only a master could think of executing. Eisenhower approved.[xvii]

This was not Patton's first experience fighting on the European continent. Twenty-six years earlier he had commanded the 1st American Tank Brigade of the American Expeditionary Forces in France. He fought at the Battle of St. Mihiel and then in the Meuse-Argonne Offensive, where he was wounded on the first day. Known as Old Blood and Guts by his men, Patton summed up his strategy for warfare when he said, "We shall attack and attack until we are exhausted, and then we shall attack again."[xviii]

While it seemed Patton could work miracles on the battlefield, he could not control the weather. The heavy rains, followed by the sleet, fog and blizzards created a logistics nightmare trying to move a hundred thousand troops, thousands of trucks, tanks, and self-propelled guns in poor visibility over roads buried beneath the ice and mud. As one officer described it, "The weather was so terrible. It was white when you looked down, white when you looked up."[xix]

The movement to Bastogne was enormously complicated. On the first two days about 100,000 troops, "accompanied by thousands of tons of supplies and equipment," turned north. Tens of thousands of jeeps, tanks, trucks, and howitzers sped toward Bastogne, 125 miles away, over roads that were sheets of mud, ice and snow. At night the drivers ignored the blackout rules and traveled at full speed with their lights on. The traffic snarled." Spending much of his time in his jeep in frigid weather, Patton rode "herd on the convoys that were suddenly turned toward Luxembourg." His communications teams did their part, laying more than 19,500 miles of wire and establishing an entirely new communications network. [xx]

Patton telephoned to Eisenhower, "General, I apologize for my slowness. This snow is God-awful. I'm sorry." "George," Ike responded, "Are you still fighting?" When Patton said he was, Ike said, "All right, that's all I've asked of you."[xxi] Events moved quickly.

110th Regiment of the American 28th Division was holding the town of Wiltz. The other two regiments of the division, the 109th and the 112th were out of contact...The two regiments of the 106th Infantry Division were cut off and surrounded, but were still fighting and were being supplied by air. Eventually, however, all members of these regiments were killed or captured.[xxii]

The 101st Airborne Division was ordered from its reserve position in France, to Bastogne, to hold at all costs. Within days the 101st, along with "one combat command of the 9th Armored Division, one combat command of the 10th Armored Division, and elements of the 28th Infantry Division,"[xxiii] were surrounded by the Germans.

For a few short days, it looked like the German gamble might pay off. All that stood in the way of the German advance to the major roads and port to the west were a few American pockets of resistance. By the ferocity of enemy engagement, it became clear that the main effort was now toward Bastogne.[xxiv] At first the 101st was well armed and supplied, engaging the Germans in the fierce fighting, "knock[ing] out 55 enemy tanks" in one day alone.[xxv]

But the intensity of battle was quickly depleting resources. Food and ammunition were running dangerously low and without resupply and reinforcements the Americans could not last past Christmas. The Germans demanded the Americans surrender to which Brigadier General Anthony McAuliffe, the commanding general of the 101st, bluntly responded, "Nuts!" The word did not translate well and it had to be clarified for the Germans that "nuts" in this case meant "no."[xxvi]

Patton, a deeply religious man despite his tendency toward profanity even while praying, decided to take his case to the highest power using as his intermediary the Chaplain of the Third Army, Father (Colonel) James O'Neill.[xxvii] During the early December heavy rains Patton summoned Chaplain O'Neill into his office. "Chaplain, I want you to publish a prayer for good weather. I'm tired of these soldiers having to fight mud and floods as well as Germans. See if we can't get God to work on our side."

Father O'Neill responded, "Sir, it's going to take a pretty thick rug for that kind of praying." Patton responded, "I don't care if it takes the flying carpet. I want the praying done." Again, the Chaplain tried to object. "May I say, General, that it usually isn't a customary thing among men of my profession to pray for clear weather to kill fellow men."

Patton was undeterred. "Chaplain, are you teaching me theology or are you Chaplain of the Third Army? I want a prayer." So Chaplain O'Neill wrote a prayer asking God to stop the rains:

> *"Almighty and most merciful Father, we humbly beseech Thee, of Thy great goodness, to restrain these immoderate rains with which we have had to contend. Grant us fair weather for Battle. Graciously hearken to us as soldiers who call upon Thee that, armed with Thy power, we may advance from victory to victory, and crush the oppression and wickedness of our enemies, and establish Thy justice among men and nations. Amen."*

The rains stopped. But the good weather didn't last, replaced by freezing temperatures and a raging blizzard. Patton was not discouraged. He ordered the prayer distributed to all Third Army troops on wallet-sized cards three days before Christmas. When informed by his Chief of Staff that the prayer was to stop the earlier rains, not the current heavy snows, Patton replied, "Oh, the Lord won't mind. He knows we're too busy right now killing Germans to print another prayer."xxviii

On one side of Patton's prayer card was his plea for fair weather. On the other side was his holiday message on the eve of battle.

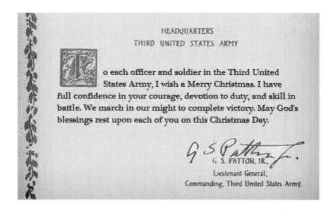

HEADQUARTERS
THIRD UNITED STATES ARMY

o each officer and soldier in the Third United States Army, I wish a Merry Christmas. I have full confidence in your courage, devotion to duty, and skill in battle. We march in our might to complete victory. May God's blessings rest upon each of you on this Christmas Day.

G. S. PATTON, JR.
Lieutenant General,
Commanding, Third United States Army.

Just for good measure, two days before Christmas Patton visited an ancient Roman Catholic chapel in Luxembourg City. Patton was Episcopalian but that did not stop him. He approached the altar, took off his helmet and knelt down to pray. "Sir, this is Patton talking. The last fourteen days have been straight hell. Rain, snow, rain, more snow — and I'm beginning to wonder what's going on in your headquarters. Whose side are you on, anyway?"xxix

Admittedly it wasn't the most pious prayer but still it was sincere in its desperation. Patton complained that God had been cooperative with fine weather for the campaigns in

Africa, Sicily and France but not so much lately. Had he offended God in some way, he wondered. He concluded:

> *"Sir I am not an unreasonable man; I am not going to ask You for the impossible. I do not even insist on a miracle, for all I request is four days of clear weather. Give me four clear days so that my planes can fly, so that my fighter-bombers can bomb and strafe, so that my reconnaissance may pick out targets for my magnificent artillery. Give me four days of sunshine to dry this blasted mud, so that my tanks may roll, so that ammunition and rations may be taken to my hungry, ill-equipped infantry. I need these four days to send von Rundstedt and his godless army to their Valhalla. I am sick of this unnecessary butchery of American youth, and in exchange for four days of fighting weather, I will deliver You enough Krauts to keep your bookkeepers months behind in their work. Amen"* xxx

Apparently, God heard Patton's prayers.

> *At the Third Army Staff briefing on the morning of 23 December the G-3 Air Officer, Lieutenant Colonel Pat Murray, made one of the finest speeches possible. He said that his weather report showed that there would be fair flying weather by 1000, and that the next day also should be clear...The weather did begin to clear on 23 December, the first time in weeks and sunrise on 24 December was the most beautiful any of us had ever seen, because it meant so much...Then our planes came, and that made the day perfect. Hundreds and hundreds, they laced the skies until the vapor trails formed a white mist almost as thick as the ground mist that had been keeping them earthbound for so long.* xxxi

The delighted Patton awarded Chaplain O'Neill the bronze star, praising him as "The most popular man in this Headquarters...[standing] in good with the Lord and soldiers."[xxxii]

Patton wrote in his journal, "Christmas dawned clear and cold; lovely weather for killing Germans, although the thought seemed somewhat at variance with the spirit of the day."[xxxiii] The day after Christmas, elements of the Third Army broke through enemy lines to rescue the 101st at Bastogne, ending the siege without a day to spare. When the first American tanks arrived on the 26th, McAuliffe ordered his officers to be well-dressed and clean shaven when they drove out to greet Patton's forces. One of Patton's officers climbed out of a tank and saluted McAuliffe, asking, "How are you, General?" The General responded, "Gee, I am mighty glad to see you."[xxxiv]

Patton wrote to his wife, Beatrice, on December 29, "The relief of Bastogne is the most brilliant operation we have thus far performed and is in my opinion the outstanding achievement of this war. Now the enemy must dance to our tune, not we to his."[xxxv] Having stopped the German advance, Patton and his mighty Third Army were now on a mad roll east to Germany.

At the end of the operation, Patton compiled a detailed report of this battlefield game-changer. Organized much like a diary, the report begins on December 12, 1944, four days before the German break-through in the Ardennes. The report continues, on a day-to-day basis, to describe the ongoing planning, logistical and operational efforts of the Third Army to save the 101st while stopping the German push west. The report concludes on January 16, 1945 with Patton giving a final assessment of losses, operational and logistical challenges.

A copy of <u>Notes on Bastogne Operation</u>, signed by General George S. Patton Jr. on January 16, 1945, is now stored at the National Archives outside Washington, D.C.[xxxvi] It has been transcribed verbatim and published here, fittingly, on its 75th anniversary. We have also included annotations, an introduction and index to provide context, clarity and ease of research.

Aleksandra Rohde
Editor-in-Chief, Dale Street Books
November 2019

---

[i] Werner Kreipe, <u>Personal Diary of Gen. Fl. Kreipe, Chief of the Luftwaffe General Staff during the Period 22 July - 2 November 1944</u>, trans. Max Franke (manuscript format) (Army Heritage and Education Center, Carlisle, Pennsylvania: Foreign Military Studies, Call Number D739 .F6713 no. P-069), diary entry for September 16, 1944.

[ii] Ibid.

[iii] Hugh M. Cole, <u>The Ardennes: Battle of the Bulge</u>, United States Army in World War II Series (Washington, D.C.: Office of the Chief of Military History Department of the Army, 1965), p. 2. "On the Eastern and Western Fronts the combined German losses during June, July, and August had totaled at least 1,200,000 dead, wounded, and missing. The rapid Allied advances in the west had cooped up an additional 230,000 troops in positions from which they would emerge only to surrender. Losses in materiel were in keeping with those in fighting manpower."

iv Stanley Weintraub, "Patton's Last Christmas," MHQ, 19, No. 2 (Winter 2007), p. 9.

v Marvin D. Kays, Weather Effects during the Battle of the Bulge and the Normandy Invasion (White Sands Missile Range, NM: U.S. Army Electronics Research and Development Command, 1982), p. 9.

vi Major James O. Kievit, Operational Art in the 1944 Ardennes Campaign (U.S. Army Command and General Staff College, Fort Leavenworth, Kansas: School of Advanced Military Studies, 1987), p. 7. "By early December, after many delays, the German forces were finally concentrated in the Eiffel Region between Cologne, Koblenz, and Trier. Aware that in many situations air power had proven to be the Allied tactical center of gravity, and recognizing that despite its best efforts the Luftwaffe would be unable to gain and maintain air superiority over the battlefield, the Germans waited for weather that would ground the Allied air forces."

vii Kays, p. 10. "The German selection of a target date for the commencement of the Ardennes Offensive was made on the prediction of poor flying weather. This type of weather had a useful side effect during the rupture of the American lines, since it veiled the attacker with fog and mist..."

viii Colonel Robert S. Allen, Lucky Forward: The History of General George Patton's Third U.S. Army (New York: Macfadden-Bartell, 1965), p. 168.

ix Ibid., p. 169.

x Ibid., p. 165.

xi Ibid., p. 163.

xii Stanley P. Hirshon, General Patton: A Soldier's Life (New York: Perennial, 2003), p. 570.

xiii Ibid.

xiv Dwight D. Eisenhower, <u>The Papers of Dwight David Eisenhower</u>, The War Years Series, Vol. II (Baltimore and London: The Johns Hopkins Press, 1970), p. 939.

xv Stanley Weintraub, <u>11 Days in December: Christmas at the Bulge, 1944</u> (New York: Free Press, 2006), p. 67.

xvi Brenton G. Wallace, <u>Patton and His Third Army</u> (Nashville: The Battery Press, 1981), p. 150.

xvii Martin Blumenson, <u>The Patton Papers 1940-1945</u> (Boston: Houghton Mifflin Company, 1957), p. 600.

xviii "George S. Patton," History.com, updated July 1, 2019.

xix Weintraub, "Patton's Last Christmas," p. 13.

xx Hirshon, p. 584.

xxi Ibid., p. 11.

xxii Wallace, p. 156.

xxiii Ibid.

xxiv Ibid., pp. 156, 157.

xxv Ibid., p. 157.

xxvi Ladislas Farago, <u>Patton Ordeal and Triumph</u> (New York: Ivan Obolensky, Inc., 1964), p. 717.

xxvii George S. Patton, Jr., <u>War as I Knew It</u>, ed. Rick Atkinson (Boston and New York: Houghton Mifflin Company, 1947), pp. 184, 185.

xxviii Allen, pp. 180, 181.

xxix <u>Battleground Luxembourg: Remember 44 The Bulge</u> (Luxembourg: Luxembourg National Tourist Office, 1993), p. 17.

xxx Ibid., p. 18.

xxxi Wallace, p. 158.

xxxii Patton, p. 186.

xxxiii Patton, p. 202.

xxxiv Weintraub, "Patton's Last Christmas," p. 15.

xxxv Blumenson, p. 608.

xxxvi Notes on Bastogne Operation, WWII Operations Reports 1940-48 Third Army (College Park, MD: National Archives, January 16, 1945). RG 407, Box 1572, Folder 103-0.5.

MOVEMENTS THIRD ARMY UNITS TO BASTOGNE OPERATION

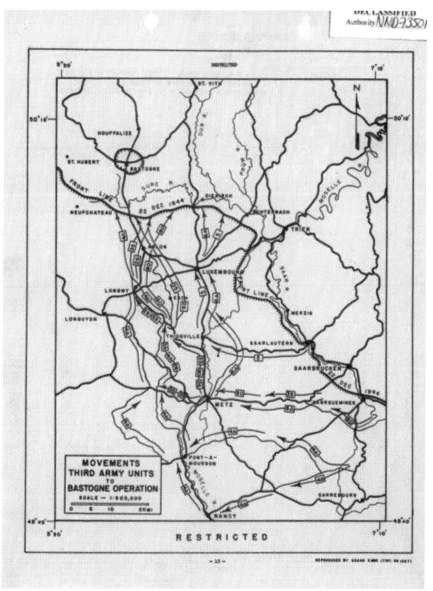

Original map appended to Patton's Notes on Bastogne Operation

January 16, 1945

NOTES ON BASTOGNE OPERATION

By December 10, 1944, the Saar Offensive of the Third Army, begun on November 8, had progressed to the point where the XX Corps had forced a crossing of the Saar at SAARLAUTERN, using the 90th and 95th Infantry Divisions, and had the 5th Infantry and 10th Armored Divisions prepared to exploit the impending break-through of the Siegfried Line in that town. The left of the Corps from REMICH to MERZIG was covered by a Task Force consisting of the 3rd Cavalry Group Reinforced, Colonel Polk commanding.

In the XII Corps zone the crossing over the Saar had been forced and the Corps was attacking in a northeasterly direction parallel to the BLIES River.

December 12, 1944

As a result of the meeting with General Spaatz, General Doolittle, General Vandenberg, General Weyland and myself, a definite scheme for the rupture of the Siegfried Line in the vicinity of ZWEIBRUCKEN-KAISERSLAUTERN by a three day air blitz, followed immediately by a ground assault had been arranged, with target date the 19th of December.

In XII Corps, the 87th Division had relieved 26th Division east of the SARREGUEMINES, and the latter had assembled at METZ and taken over the training of 4,000 replacements secured through a 5% cut in the overhead of all Corps and Army troops in the Third Army.

1

The 5th and 80th Divisions were up to strength but the Army as a whole was 12,000 short. All divisions were ordered to cannibalize headquarters and anti-tank gun sections to provide infantry riflemen.

December 16, 1944

In the XX Corps, the 5th Infantry Division began to relieve the 95th Division in SAARLAUTERN, preparatory to the final assault for a break of the Siegfried Line. It was then to attack NE in the Corps zone supported by the 10th Armored Division.

Due to heavy enemy resistance, the date of the air blitz at ZWEIBRUCKEN was moved to December 21 to assure the arrival of ground troops within assaulting distance of the Siegfried Line in time for this date. The XII Corps started to place the 80th Infantry and 4th Armored in line abreast of the 87th Infantry Division.

The III Corps, consisting of the 26th and 6th Armored Divisions, which had become operational December 15, initiated a reconnaissance with a view to passing through the 35th Infantry Division, XII Corps, immediately subsequent to the blitz.

Orders were issued for movement of Headquarters Third Army to ST. AVOLD on December 19.

Orders were received from Twelfth Army Group directing the 10th Armored Division be temporarily attached to VIII Corps, First Army, to counter a serious attempt at a break-through on the part of the enemy, this movement to be initiated December 17.

December 18, 1944

At the direction of the Army Group Commander I reported to his Headquarters LUXEMBOURG, accompanied by G-2, G-3, and G-4 of the Third Army. The situation of the enemy break-through, as then known, was explained.

General Bradley* asked when I could intervene. I stated I could do so with three divisions very shortly. I then telephoned the Chief of Staff Third Army and directed that the attack of the 4th Armored and 8th Infantry Divisions be halted and sufficient transportation to move the 80th Division any time after dawn of the 19th be collected. That the 4th Armored Division be prepared to move the night 18-19 December. Also to notify the XIX Tactical Air Command that the blitz was off for the present.

General Bradley called at 2200 hours and stated that the situation was worse than it had been at noon and directed that the troops as per previous paragraph be moved as rapidly as possible. Also that General Milliken move forward echelon of his headquarters to the front. I suggested ARLON. This was approved. General Bradley further ordered that General Milliken report in person to the Chief of Staff Twelfth Army Group on the morning of the 19th; and that I, accompanied by one staff officer, meet General Bradley for a conference with General Eisenhower at VERDUN at 1100 the same date.

One Combat Command of the 4th Armored moved at midnight on LONGWY, followed by remainder of division at dawn. The 80th Infantry started to move on LUXEMBOURG at dawn December 19. The G-4 of the Twelfth Army Group facilitated these operations by a rapid collection of truck companies from Com. Z.

December 19, 1944

Meeting of all Corps Commanders and the Commanding General of the XIX Tactical Air Command and the General Staff of the Third Army was called at 0800. The new situation was explained. I stated that the reputation of the Third Army and XIX Tactical Air Command for speed and effectiveness resulted from the efficiency of the officers

---

* General Omar N. Bradley, Commander, 12th Army Group.

present, and that I counted upon them for even greater successes.

On the assumption that VIII Corps would be assigned to Third Army, a plan for the employment of III and VIII Corps was drawn up. Three possible lines of attack were envisaged: NEUFCHATEAU-ST. HUBERT; ARLON-BASTOGNE; LUXEMBOURG-DIEKIRCH-ST.VITH.

A brief telephone code between myself and the Chief of Staff Third Army was drawn up.

Left for VERDUN at 0930, arriving at 1045.

As a result of the conference, the Supreme Commander directed that the Sixth Army Group take over the southern front as far north as the southern boundary of the XX Corps, Third Army; the 6th Armored Division to stay in the SAARBRUCKEN area until relieved by elements of the [Seventh]* Army. The 87th and 42nd Infantry Divisions of the Third Army to pass to the [Seventh] Army.

At this moment, it seemed to me probable that the Third Army in its new role would be constituted as follows:

VIII Corps (General Middleton) in vicinity of NEUFCHATEAU—101st Airborne Division, and elements of 28th Infantry, 9th and 10th Armored Divisions, and 106th Infantry Division, plus Corps troops. III Corps (General Milliken) in vicinity of ARLON—26th Infantry, 80th Infantry, and 4th Armored Divisions. The XII Corps (General Eddy) to be assembled in vicinity of LUXEMBOURG—consisting of 35th, 4th, and 5th Infantry Divisions, and elements of the 9th and 10th Armored Divisions. The XX Corps (General Walker) in vicinity of THIONVILLE—90th AND 95th Infantry Divisions, 6th Armored Division when relieved by [Seventh] Army, and Task Force Polk.

In reply to a question from General Eisenhower as to when the Third Army could attack to the north, I stated it could attack with III Corps on the 23rd of December.

After the meeting at VERDUN, I called Chief of Staff Third Army on phone and gave following instructions: 26th

---

* Patton had abbreviated "Seventh" as "7th."

Infantry Division to be moved December 20 to vicinity of
ARLON, advanced detachments to move at once. The XII
Corps to disengage, and Corps Headquarters and artillery
to move to vicinity of LUXEMBOURG 21st of December,
leaving a working headquarters at old location until such
time as it could be relieved by XV Corps, [Seventh] Army.
35th Infantry Division to be withdrawn from line and
assembled at METZ. Tactical Echelon Third Army
Headquarters to move on LUXEMBOURG 20th of
December. Forward Echelon III Corps to move in vicinity of
ARLON at once.

December 20, 1944

     I visited Twelfth Army Group at LUXEMBOURG, then
the Commanding Generals of the III and VIII Corps and 4th
Armored Division at ARLON, later visited Headquarters 4th
and 26th Infantry Divisions, 9th and 10th Armored
Divisions, and the advanced echelon 80th Division which
had just reached LUXEMBOURG.
     As it was apparent that for the present the VIII Corps
had no offensive power, it was directed to hold BASTOGNE
with the 101st Airborne Division and following
attachments: one CC* of the 9th Armored and one CC of the
10th Armored Division; the 705th TD† Battalion, less one

---

* Combat command. "A Combat Command was a
combined-arms military organization of comparable size to
a brigade or regiment employed by armored forces of the
United States Army from 1942 until 1963. The structure of
combat commands was task-organized and so the forces
assigned to a combat command often varied from mission
to mission. Combat Command is most often abbreviated by
one of the related derivative notations: CCA, or CC-A or CC
A; CCB, or CC-B or CC B; CCC, or CC-C or CC C (an older
convention for "reserve formation"); and CCR, or CC-R or
CC R (for Combat Command Reserve)."
† Tank destroyer.

company; and some Corps Artillery. Remainder of the Corps to fall back, using delaying action and demolitions.

The III Corps is to attack with the purpose of relieving BASTOGNE on 22nd of December 0600. The Commanding General 10th Armored Division was directed to take temporary command of XII Corps pending arrival of that Headquarters. Also to incorporate in his unit one CC of the 9th Armored Division in the vicinity of LUXEMBOURG. The Commanding General of the 9th Armored Division with his headquarters was sent to VIII Corps to take over command of two combat commands of the 9th Armored and one combat command of the 10th Armored Division.

Through the Chief of Staff Third Army arranged for immediate movement to new theater of combat of all self-propelled tank destroyer battalions and separate tank battalions, necessary ammunition, engineers, and hospitals.

Also, that the 5th Division be disengaged at SAARLAUTERN and be moved to LUXEMBOURG at once. NOTE: The 10th Infantry of the 5th Division actually reached LUXEMBOURG at midnight this date, and one company of tank destroyers of the 818th TD Battalion, which had been in combat east of the Saar River in the morning, opened fire on the enemy north of the Sauer River that night, having marched in the meantime 69 miles.

It is noteworthy that all the operations, including plans for attack executed on the 22nd of December, were done by personal conference or by telephone, and that the highly complicated road and supply movements were only made possible by the old and very experienced General Staff of the Third Army and the high discipline and devotion to duty of all the units involved.

NOTES ON BASTOGNE OPERATION

December 21, 1944

U.S. losses during Saar Operation from November 8th to midnight December 21st amounted to 29,688 killed, wounded, and missing. During the same period, enemy opposed to the Third Army lost 40,265 Prisoners of War or buried by our Graves Registration.

December 22, 1944

The III Corps (4th Armored, 26th, and 80th Infantry Divisions) attacked at 0600. BASTOGNE was still holding out. The 10th Infantry Regiment of the 5th Division, XII Corps, attacked NE on ECHTERNACH, driving the enemy towards the river.

December 23, 1944

The weather fine. Seven fighter-bomber groups, eleven medium-bomber groups, and one division of the 8th Air Force and elements of the RAF were up in support of the Third Army.

The III Corps continued its attack. The XII Corps continued its limited attack. The XX Corps launched an attack in the direction of SAARBURG as a diversion.

The 35th Infantry Division closed on METZ at 2400 hours.

December 24, 1944

The 6th Cavalry Group, reinforced with one company of engineers and one company of tank destroyers, moved, this date, to join the III Corps.

The III Corps continues attack. The XII Corps cleared Sauer River from DIEKIRCH inclusive to ECHTERNACH exclusive.

December 25, 1944

Clear and cold. All the air up. Visited all front line divisions. Where men were in contact and could not get hot Xmas dinner, they were served chicken sandwiches.

Exchanged the 6th Armored Division (XX Corps) with 10th Armored Division (XII Corps) effective tonight.

The 35th Infantry Division which closed at METZ on midnight the 23rd of December, absorbed 2000 replacements from the second 5% cut in Corps and Army troops of Third Army, all with less than a week's training. They will close north of ARLON at 1400 tomorrow, prepared to attack between the 26th Infantry and 4th Armored Divisions the morning of the 27th. The 80th Infantry Division passes to XII Corps at 1800, the 26th.

December 26, 1944

Combat Command "A", 9th Armored Division, serving with 10th Armored Division in XII Corps joined to 4th Armored Division this morning and attacks west of CC "R"* (Colonel Blanchard) 4th Armored Division.

Colonel Blanchard's CC "R" by a very daring attack entered BASTOGNE 1645 with one battalion of armored infantry and one battalion of tanks. We took in 40 truckloads of supplies that night, thus re-opening the supply route. Also, 22 ambulances with a total of 652 wounded were evacuated; the first night 224 went out and the remaining were evacuated the next morning.

The total time from the moment when the 4th Armored Division left the SAARBRUCKEN sector to the taking of BASTOGNE was seven days; the distance covered was 120 miles; the distances gained by combat during four days was 16 miles. In addition to the 4th Armored Division, the 318th Infantry (less 3rd Battalion) of the 80th Division and Combat Command "A" of the 9th Armored Division

---

* Combat command reserve.

should be given special credit for the penetration into
BASTOGNE.

The 6th Armored Division closed on LUXEMBOURG.
The 87th Infantry and 17th Airborne and 11th Armored
Divisions are near REIMS in SHAEF Reserve. The Third
Army requested their assignment.

December 28, 1944

General Bradley explained further operations for a
future continuation of the Army Group offensive action.

The 11th Armored and 87th Infantry Divisions
released to Third Army and assigned to the VIII Corps.

December 29, 1944

Started 11th Armored and 87th Infantry Divisions on
NEUFCHATEAU. They should close by 2400 and will attack
west of BASTOGNE on HOUFFALIZE at 0800 December
30th.

6th Armored Division closed north of ARLON,
preparatory to attacking on the axis BASTOGNE-ST. VITH
on the 31st.

December 30, 1944

The 11th Armored Division on the right and the 87th
Infantry Division on the left jumped off at 0800 and ran
into the flank of a German counterattack headed SE to cut
off BASTOGNE. The German attack consisted of the 130th
Panzer Lehr Division and the 26th Volksgrenadier Division.
Our attack stopped them and turned them back. At the
same time on the other flank of the BASTOGNE bulge, the
35th and 26th Infantry Divisions were attacked by the 1st
SS Panzer Division and the 167th Volksgrenadier Division.
The artillery of the 4th Armored Division came to the help of
the 35th Infantry Division, and the enemy was repulsed

with the loss of 55 tanks. This repulse was largely aided by the action of the XIX Tactical Air Command which was able to fly most of the day despite very bad weather. The 101st Airborne Division also repulsed a counterattack from the NW.

Unquestionably, this was a critical day of the operation, as there was a concerted effort on the part of the Germans, using at least five divisions, to again isolate BASTOGNE.

Twenty-one Germans wearing U.S. uniforms were killed in battle.

Army Commander entered BASTOGNE and decorated Brigadier General McAuliffe.

December 31, 1944

Very bad weather with snow and sleet. Tractors could not be used to pull guns. Necessary to use the diamond-six trucks.

Germans continued to counterattack strongly, but the 6th Armored Division attacked as planned and made 4 kilometers on its axis. The enemy counterattacked 17 times today—11 repulsed with heavy losses to the enemy. We also sustained casualties, particularly in the case of the 11th Armored Division which is very green.

The 17th Airborne Division was released to the Third Army and is being replaced at REIMS by the 28th Infantry Division less one regiment still with the First Army.

January 1, 1945

At 0001 all guns of Third Army fired a New Year's greeting on the enemy for twenty minutes—heavy casualties inflicted.

Germans have formed a definite pocket in woods SE of BASTOGNE from which they seriously threaten our line of supply and bring the principal road under machine gun and mortar fire. It will be necessary to evict them.

The 6th Armored Division continued to advance. All other units made little to no progress.

The VII Corps, First Army, will initiate an attack on HOUFFALIZE from the north in the morning. This should take some pressure from the Third Army.

The 17th Airborne Division ordered to attack through 11th Armored Division at 1200, January 3.

January 3, 1945

87th Infantry Division gained on the left. The 11th Armored repulsed a strong counterattack in the center but is badly disorganized and needs a few days out of the line. Due to slippery conditions of the roads, the 17th Airborne Division was unable to attack through the 11th Armored Division as planned.

January 4, 1945

The 17th Airborne Division attacked through 11th Armored Division and ran into violent resistance, suffering heavy losses due to inexperience. The individual fighting of the men was excellent.

If the 94th Infantry Division is released to the Third Army, it will replace the 90th Infantry Division in the XX Corps, and the 90th Division will be sent to the III Corps for the purpose of cleaning pocket SE of BASTOGNE.

January 5, 1945

The 94th Infantry Division, less one Combat Team, was cleared to the Third Army at 1730. Moves to THIONVILLE at once.

January 6, 1945

Final details for employment of 90th Infantry Division settled. It will attack on January 9th through 26th Infantry Division in a northwesterly direction along ridge road, cutting base of salient. The 26th Infantry Division, 6th Cavalry Group Task Force, the 35th Infantry Division and 6th Armored Division are attacking concentrically along the perimeter of the pocket. One thousand guns are supporting the attack, some firing in prolongation and others at right angles to the main effort to insure dispersion both ways.

A deception detachment was left in XX Corps to keep up 90th Infantry Division radio net.

Enemy attacked three times today without success and in little force. I fear he is withdrawing. No flying due to bad weather.

January 7, 1945

The 319th Regiment of the 80th Infantry Division in a night attack secured the town of DAHL with surprisingly small casualties. This attack not only kept the enemy off balance but also protects right flank of the 26th Infantry Division.

Some rumors of an attack against the northern front of the XII Corps in direction of DIEKIRCH. Measures taken to establish road blocks and minefields.

January 8, 1945

I determined to renew attack on HOUFFALIZE on 9th by adding to the present stalled attack of the 87th Infantry and 17th Airborne Divisions, a new attack by the 101st Airborne and the 4th Armored Divisions.

The attack in the morning will comprise eight divisions. The VIII Corps from left to right—87th Infantry,

17th and 101st Airborne Divisions, and 4th Armored Division. The III Corps—6th Armored, 35th Infantry, 90th Infantry, and 26th Infantry Divisions.

The 319th Regiment of the 80th Infantry Division repulsed a heavy counterattack of three battalions of Germans supported by tanks. We lost 9 men killed and 50 wounded. More than 300 German dead counted on the snow.

Due to severe fighting heretofore sustained, the attack of the 87th Infantry Division and the 17th Airborne Division will be of limited intensity but will retain the initiative.

Continued rumors of a German counteroffensive in the vicinity of SAARBRUCKEN.

January 9, 1945

Limited flying weather. The attack of the VIII and III Corps jumped off as planned. The 90th Infantry Division, making the main effort, received heavy casualties from artillery and rocket fire just after the jump off, but advanced 2½ kilometers. The 101st Airborne and 4th Armored Divisions moved forward, the former securing the woods west of NOVILLE. The remaining units in the two corps made very limited progress.

The rumors about the German counteroffensive from the vicinity of SAARBRUCKEN continue.

January 10, 1945

Higher authority decided that an armored division should be withdrawn from the line as a precautionary measure against the possible German attack from SAARBRUCKEN.

The attack of the 101st Airborne and 4th Armored Divisions was therefore called off at noon, and the 4th Armored will withdraw during darkness. At the same time the 101st Airborne Division and the 6th Armored Division will link up. The entire VIII Corps will limit offensive operations to vigorous patrolling. III Corps continues attack. All the arrangements for this change were made by personal contact between the Army Commander and Corps and Divisions involved.

All elements of the III Corps, particularly the 90th Infantry Division, made fair progress. A column of German guns and armor, attempting to withdraw in front of the 90th Infantry Division, was brought under artillery fire and also attacked by fighter-bombers from the XIX Tactical Air Command with good results.

General Bradley secured authority to advance the 9th Armored and 8th Armored Divisions, now on the Meuse, to the Moselle between PONT A MOUSSON and THIONVILLE. This, with the presence of the 4th Armored Division south of LUXEMBOURG, makes the situation, so far as a German attack from SAARBRUCKEN is concerned, very satisfactory.

January 11, 1945

III Corps making fair progress and securing a large number of prisoners.

Visited XX Corps to arrange plans for attacking Germans should they initiate offensive near SAARBRUCKEN. The key to this situation is ST. AVOLD. As long as we hold there and attack from there, the Germans cannot move effectively in any direction.

January 12, 1945

The VIII Corps resumes attack on HOUFFALIZE as follows from west to east: 87th Infantry, 17th Airborne, 11th Armored, and 101st Airborne Divisions.

The III Corps continues attack for the final mopping up of the salient, SE of BASTOGNE.

14

NOTES ON BASTOGNE OPERATION

January 13, 1945

Attitude of troops completely changed. They now have full confidence that they are pursuing a defeated enemy. This in spite of the fact that the Germans north and northeast of BASTOGNE are resisting viciously in order to preserve their escape routes.

Plan to withdraw one RCT* of the 87th Infantry Division from VIII Corps and assign it to XII Corps preparatory to attacking with XII Corps north from DIEKIRCH.

January 14, 1945

The VIII Corps attacked with great effectiveness and is very close to contact with First Army in the vicinity of HOUFFALIZE.

January 15, 1945

Moving remainder of the 87th Infantry Division and assigning both 87th Infantry and 4th Armored Divisions to XII Corps. This Corps will attack north from DIEKIRCH on ST. VITH on the 18th.

January 16, 1945

At 0905, 41st Cavalry of the 11th Armored Division made contact with 41st Infantry of the 2nd Armored Division in HOUFFALIZE, thus terminating the BASTOGNE operation so far as the Third Army is concerned.

During the period of this operation, the Third Army utilized a total of 17 divisions and lost in killed, wounded, and missing, 24,598 men. In the same period the Germans utilized 20 divisions and lost a total of 18,051 in prisoners of war and enemy buried by us. Their estimated casualties,

---

* Regimental combat team.

excluding non-battle, for this period amount to 103,900 as follows: 16,400 prisoners of war; 24,200 killed; 63,200 wounded. We believe that these figures are low.

On 18 December 1944 Army engineer troops and supplies were massed behind the XII Corps prepared to support the main effort of the Third Army to breach the Siegfried Line in the Sarreguemines area. By 22 December 1944 these same engineer troops were redisposed in an area extending from LUXEMBOURG on the east to VIRTON on the west, operating in close support of two Corps on offensive assignments and one Corps on defensive assignments, and thousands of tons of bridging and demolitions were moving north and west to new supply dumps in the ESCH-ARLON area. From 22 December 1944 to 16 January 1945 more than 2800 miles of roads were reconnoitered and maintained. Continuous dense traffic, combined with drifting snows, made this task a gigantic one. During this same period, the installation and dismantling of road blocks and tactical demolitions expended over 100,000 A.T. mines* and 200,000 pounds of TNT. Bridging presented no problems in the initial phase of action, but toward the middle of January had again become a major function.

As of the 18th of December 1944, the major preponderance of Third Army ordnance troops, ammunition, and supplies, were concentrated on the TOUL-NANCY-SARREGUEMINES axis to support the projected attack of the XII Corps.

With the change of direction of the attack to the north, all incoming ammunition was diverted to existing ASP's† in the LONGWY-ESCH area and new ASP's established. By rail and truck companies an average of 4,500 tons of ammunition was moved per day, truck companies traveling in one week 462,000 miles in the hauling of ammunition alone. During this period—

---

* Anti-tank mines.

† Ammunition supply point.

December 22nd to January 16th—the average consumption of ammunition per day in the Army area averaged 3,500 tons.

Maintenance requirements were met by moving ordnance units in coordination with the movement of combat units they had previously serviced. Replacement, new issue, and other ordnance supply issues were handled generally in the same manner as the ammunition supply, necessitating the movement of 45,000 tons of replacement equipment and spare parts, with the issue to troops during this period of 1,940 general purpose vehicles, 814 combat vehicles and 152 artillery weapons as replacements.

The fighting quality of American troops never reached a higher level than in this operation. Neither intolerable weather or the best troops in the possession of the Germans were able to stop them or prevent their supply.

(Sgd)
G.S. Patton, Jr.,
Lieut. General, U.S. Army,
Commanding.

McAULIFFE AND O'NEILL AWARDS*

HEADQUARTERS
THIRD UNITED STATES ARMY
APO 403

GENERAL ORDERS

14 January 1945.

NUMBER   14

SECTION. I – Award of Distinguished Service Cross.
SECTION II – Award of Bronze Star Medal.

I. AWARD OF DISTINGUISHED SERVICE CROSS – By Direction of the President and under the provisions of Sec I, Cir No. 32, Hq ETO US Army, 20 March 1944, as amended by Sec I, Cir No. 56, Hq ETO US Army, 27 May 1944, the award of the Distinguished Service Cross to the following named officers on 30 December 1944 is announced:

Brigadier General ANTHONY C McAULIFFE, 012263, United States Army, 101st Airborne Division, United States Army. For extraordinary heroism in connection with military operations against an armed enemy. During the period 17 December to 26 December 1944, General McAULIFFE was in command of the 101st Airborne Division during the siege of BASTOGNE, BELGIUM, by overwhelming enemy forces. Though the city was completely surrounded by the enemy, the spirit of the defending troops under this officer's inspiring, gallant leadership never wavered. Their courageous stand is epic. General McAULIFFE continuously exposed himself to enemy bombing, strafing, and armored and infantry attacks to personally direct his troops, utterly disregarding his own safety. His courage, fearless determination and inspiring, heroic leadership exemplify the highest traditions of the military forces of the United States.

"Brigadier General ANTHONY C. McAULIFFE, 012263, United States Army, 101st Airborne Division, United States Army. For extraordinary heroism in connection with military operations against an armed enemy. During the period 17 December to 26 December 1944, General McAULIFFE was in command of the 101st Airborne Division during the siege of BASTOGNE, BELGIUM, by overwhelming enemy forces. Though the city was completely surrounded by the enemy, the spirit of the defending troops under this officer's inspiring, gallant leadership never wavered. Their courageous stand is epic. General McAULIFFE continuously exposed himself to enemy bombing, strafing, and armored and infantry attacks to personally direct his troops, utterly disregarding his own safety. His courage, fearless determination and inspiring, heroic leadership exemplify the highest traditions of the military forces of the United States."

*National Archives, College Park, MD, "Records of the Adjutant General's Office: Awards and Decorations." RG 407, Box 1586, Folder 103.1-6.

IV. <u>AWARD OF BRONZE STAR MEDAL</u> - By Direction of the President and under the provisions of Sec I, Cir 32, Hq ETO US Army, 20 Mar 1944, as amended by Sec I, Cir 56,
Hq ETO US Army, 27 May 1944, a Bronze Star Medal is awarded to:

Chaplain (Colonel) JAMES H O'NEILL, 016370, Corps of Chaplains, Headquarters
Third United States Army. For meritorious service in connection with military
operations against an enemy of the United States in FRANCE from 15 September 1944
to 21 December 1944.

By command of Lieutenant General PATTON:

HOBART R. GAY,
Brigadier General, U. S. Army,
Chief of Staff.

OFFICIAL

*"Chaplain (Colonel) James H. O'Neill, 016379, Corps of
Chaplains, Headquarters, Third United States Army. For
meritorious service in connection with military operations against
an enemy of the United States in FRANCE from 15 September
1944 to 21 December 1944."*

BIBLIOGRAPHY

Allen, Robert A. Lucky Forward: The History of General
George Patton's Third U.S. Army. New York:
Macfadden-Bartell, 1965.

Blumenson, Martin. Patton: The Man Behind the
Legend, 1885-1945. New York: Quill - William
Morrow, 1985.

-------. The Patton Papers 1940-1945. Boston:
Houghton Mifflin Company, 1957.

Cole, Hugh M. The Ardennes: Battle of the Bulge.
United States Army in World War II Series.
Washington, D.C.: Office of the Chief of Military
History Department of the Army, 1965.

D'Este, Carlo. Patton: A Genius for War. New York:
HarperPerennial, 1996.

Eisenhower, Dwight D. The Papers of Dwight David
Eisenhower. The War Years Series, Vol. II.
Baltimore and London: The Johns Hopkins Press,
1970.

Farago, Ladislas. Patton Ordeal and Triumph. New
York: Ivan Obolensky, Inc., 1964.

Hirshson, Stanley P. General Patton: A Soldier's Life.
New York: Perennial, 2003.

Kievit, James O. "Operational Art in the 1944 Ardennes
Campaign." U.S. Army Command and General
Staff College, Fort Leavenworth, Kansas: School
of Advanced Military Studies, 1987.

Kreipe, Werner, "Personal Diary of [General der Flieger]
Kreipe, Chief of the Luftwaffe General Staff
during the period 22 July - 2 November 1944.
Trans. Max Franke. (Manuscript format)
Carlisle, Penn.: Army Heritage and Education
Center, Foreign Military Studies, Call Number
D739 .F6713 no. P-069.

Kays, Marvin D. Weather Effects during the Battle of
the Bulge and the Normandy Invasion. White

Sands Missile Range, NM: U.S. Army Electronics Research and Development Command: Atmospheric Sciences Laboratory, 1982.

Patton, George S. Jr. 304th American Brigade at St. Mihiel: Operations of the 304th Tank Brigade, September 12th to 15th, 1918. Appendix 4 to "Rockenbach Report," by Samuel D. Rockenbach, originally titled, Operations of the Tank Corps A.E.F. with the 1st American Army at St. Mihiel and in the Argonne Sept. 11th to Nov. 11th, 1918 and with the British E.F. Sept. 18th to November, 1918. Carlisle, Penn.: Army Heritage and Education Center. Call Number D608 .R626 1918.

-------. Notes on Bastogne Operation. WWII Operations Reports 1940-48 Third Army. College Park, MD: National Archives. RG 407, Box 1572, Folder 103-0.5.

-------. War as I Knew It. Ed. Rick Atkinson. Boston and New York: Houghton Mifflin Company, 1947.

------- and Ranulf Compton. War Diary 1918. Silver Spring: Dale Street Books, 2018.

Rockenbach, Samuel D. Operations of the Tank Corps, A.E.F. Silver Spring: Dale Street Books, 2017.

Wallace, Brenton G. Patton and His Third Army. Nashville: The Battery Press, 1981.

Weintraub, Stanley. 11 Days in December: Christmas at the Bulge, 1944. New York: Free Press, 2006.

Weintraub, Stanley. "Patton's Last Christmas." MHQ, 19, No. 2, Winter 2007.

Battleground Luxembourg: Remember 44 The Bulge. Luxembourg: Luxembourg National Tourist Office, 1993.

"George S. Patton," History.com, updated July 1, 2019.

INDEX

705th TD (Tank Destroyer) Battalion, 5.

818th Tank TD, 6.

Ammunition, v, xii, xv, 6, 16, 17.

Antwerp, viii.

Ardennes, v, vii, ix.

Arlon, 3, 4, 5, 8, 9, 16.

Air Forces — XIX Tactical Air Command, 3, 10, 14; bombers, xv, 7, 14; 8th Air Force, 7; RAF, 7.

Armies and Corps —
    Sixth Army Group, 4.
    Twelfth Army Group, 2, 3, 5.
    First Army, ix, x, 2, 10, 11, 15.
    Third Army — Overview, ix, x, xiii, xiv, xv, xvi; feared German break through, 1, 2; Patton's bold plan, 3, 4, 5; Third Army reorganizes, changes course, moves out, 5, 6; losses during Saar Operation, 7; December 23 weather, 7; attacking Bastogne, 7, 8, 9; more reorganizing, 9, 10, 11; fighting continues, 10; fighting terminated at Bastogne, 15; details of Patton's bold plan to turn Third Army north coming to aid of First Army, 16, 17.

    Seventh Army, 4, 5.

    III Corps — organization, 2, 4, 7, 13; General Milliken, 4; plan to attack on 23 December, 4, 5, 6; attack on Bastogne, 7, 11, 13, 14.

    VII Corps, 11.

    VIII Corps — First Army, 2; assigned to Third Army, 4; General Middleton, 4; organization, 4, 6, 9, 15; at Arlon, 4, 5; no offensive power, 5; directed to hold Bastogne, 5; attack on Houffalize, 12, 14, 15.

    XV Corps, 5.

    XX Corps — crossing the Saar, 1; preparing to break Siegfried Line, 2; area of operations, 4; General Walker, 4; organization 1, 2, 4, 8, 11; diversion at Saarburg, 7; 90th Division

23

green," 10, 11;
"individual
fighting of men
was excellent," 11;
attack on
Houffalize, 14;
terminating
Bastogne
operation, 15; 41st
Cavalry of, 15.
17th Airborne—near
Reims, 9; replaced
by 28th Infantry,
10; cleaning out
German pockets of
resistance, 11, 12,
13; Houffalize, 14.
26th Infantry—plan as of
19, 20 December, 4,
5; plans for attack
on 27 December, 8;
attacked, 9;
cleaning out
German pockets of
resistance, 12, 13.
28th Infantry—surrounded
by Germans, xii;
109th Regiment,
xii; 110th
Regiment, xii;
112th Regiment,
xii; component of
reconstituted
Third Army, 4;
replacing 17th
Airborne, 10.
35th Infantry—preparing
for break in

Siegfried Line, 2;
withdrawn and
assembled at Metz,
5; closing on Metz,
7; closing north of
Arlon, 8; attacked,
9; clearing pockets
of German
resistance, 12.
42nd Infantry, 4.
80th Infantry—planning to
counter German
break, 2, 3, 4;
attacking on 22
December, 7;
passing to XII
Corps, 8; 318th
Infantry (less 3rd
Battalion) among
units given special
credit for
penetration of
Bastogne, 8, 9;
319th Regiment
secures town of
Dahl, 12; repulsed
heavy
counterattack, 13.
87th Infantry—relieving
26th Division east
of the
Sarreguemines, 1;
planning for
German break, 2, 4;
near Reims, 9;
released to Third
Army, 9; attacking
on Houffalize, 9;

Publications from

DALE STREET BOOKS

Military Strategy, Tactics and Training

Battle of Booby's Bluffs is a blunt depiction of incompetence by some American Army officers in World War I, who were unable to adapt their old-fashioned tactics to the new weapons of modern war–tanks, machine guns, stokes mortars, and airplanes. Written in the dream-sequence style of the infantry classic, Defence of Duffer's Drift, the main character is a pompous know-it-all who relives the same dream over and over until by trial and error he learns how to keep his men alive and win on the modern battlefield. Written under the pseudonym Major Single List, the anonymous author had good reason to hide his identity, given the number of feathers his amusing but highly critical book likely ruffled.

Cavalry and Tanks in Future Wars is a collection of writings by George S. Patton Jr. Patton applies his diverse experiences as a cavalry officer chasing Pancho Villa on the Mexican Border and a tank commander on the battlefields in 1918 France to defend the continued relevance of cavalry and tanks in future wars.

Defence of Duffer's Drift by Sir Ernest D. Swinton is a classic in the art of infantry tactics and required reading at many Army schools.

Diary of the Instructor in Swordsmanship is the second training manual written by George S. Patton Jr., to teach cavalry officers the proper saber tactics and techniques for mounted and dismounted engagements. (His first training manual, Saber Exercise 1914, covers the general rules while this second manual presents more detailed instructions.)

In Defense of My Saber is a collection of articles written by George S. Patton Jr. advocating for his redesigned cavalry saber. It begins in the glory days when his saber was embraced by the Army as standard issue. It ends with its ultimate decline into irrelevance after the Great War—and despite Patton's ardent pleas to the contrary.

Saber Exercise 1914 Training Manual in Swordsmanship (originally titled Saber Exercise 1914) was written by George S. Patton Jr. the year after the War Department approved his radical redesign of the cavalry saber. The redesign necessitated a fundamental change in mounted and dismounted saber work—all of which is explained in this manual.

World War I in Europe

American Expeditionary Forces in Europe 1917-1918 from the German Perspective examines the American involvement in the last days of the Great War from the German point of view. It was written by Hermann von Giehrl, a staff officer in the German Army. Von Giehrl planned the organized retreat of the German army in the face of overwhelming American forces and was therefore privy to the High Command's mindset, strategy, and plans during those final days—which he candidly shares with the reader. Also an accomplished writer, he presents a poignant picture of a once proud military facing inevitable defeat.

Battle of the Meuse-Argonne from the German Perspective, by German Army Major Hermann von Giehrl, is a military analysis of the Battle of the Meuse-Argonne from the German point of view. In Major von Giehrl's eyes, the Americans and French are the enemy. But his writing is surprisingly free of nationalistic fervor. Instead he offers an objective view of the 42 days leading up to the German surrender, written by a soldier, not a politician or apologist. Von Giehrl is candid in his assessment of the effectiveness of the French and Germans, traumatized by four long years of the modern battlefield overwhelmed by tanks, aeroplanes, machine guns, mortars and gas. By contrast, his description of the naïve but strapping young Americans as they arrived on a ravaged continent not yet having learned to fear the horrors that awaited them is truly poignant.

Operations of the Tank Corps A.E.F. is the official report of the
U.S. Army Tank Corps–how it was organized, equipped,
manned, trained and then deployed into battle in 1918
France. Commonly known as the Rockenbach Report, it
was compiled by Brigadier General Samuel D.
Rockenbach, the father of the Tank Corps and its first
Commander. Among the addendums to the main report
are an organization roster listing the units and personnel
by name assigned to the Tank Corps in September 1918;
and an operations report by Lieutenant Colonel George S.
Patton Jr., Commander of 304th Tank Brigade, on the
Battle of St. Mihiel.

War Diary 1918, contains the official war diaries kept by George
S. Patton Jr., commander of the 304th Tank Brigade and
Ranulf Compton, one of his battalion tank commanders.
These war diaries were required by the War Department to
be kept by all commanders to create a detailed history of
American operations in 1918 Europe. Patton's and
Compton's diary entries at the brigade and battalion levels
respectively, provide a candid look at early American tank
units on the Western Front. Included are Patton's
complete and unedited daily diary entries from September
1918 to the final days leading up to the Armistice in
November. Compton's daily entries begin in August as his
battalion prepares for combat at the Battle of St. Mihiel
until mid-October during the Meuse-Argonne Offensive.
Compton's diary entries are particularly important
because he is a lesser-known figure historically but one
who played a critical role in the final days of the war.
Sereno Brett, Patton's other battalion commander, had
assumed command of the brigade after Patton was
wounded the last week in September. Compton, in turn,
assumed command of all the brigade tanks at the front.
His role as commander of the fighting tanks makes his
diary entries especially valuable. Once Patton was
medically evacuated off the battlefield, his knowledge of
tank operations was strictly second-hand. But Compton
was now eyewitness to several more weeks of some of the
toughest fighting of the war. The contrast between
Patton's and Compton's diary entries is also intriguing for
another reason. On a personal level, Patton had a vested

interest in the success of the early tank, having been an early proponent and personally involved in its development. But Compton had no such investment and therefore his daily observations, in contrast to Patton's, contain a more unvarnished assessment of the early tank, recording in detail not just its strengths, but also its weaknesses.

World War II in Europe

Campaign in Poland 1939 is a previously classified analysis by U.S. military strategists at the Department of Military Art and Engineering, United States Military Academy, detailing the "Polish Campaign" instigated by the German invasion in September 1939. Included are maps showing the troop movements and engagements over the course of the four-week conflict that ended with a conquered Poland.

German Fifth Column in Poland by the Polish Ministry of Information exposes the treachery of the German population living inside Polish borders but lending clandestine assistance to the invading German Army in September 1939.

German Occupation of Poland was published by the Polish Ministry of Foreign Affairs in the first years of the war. It exposed for the first time to the world community the dire conditions in Nazi-occupied Poland with detailed reports on the summary executions of civilians, eviction of Poles from their homes, the closing of schools, synagogues and universities and the forced relocation of Jews into ghettoes.

Mass Extermination of Jews in German Occupied Poland was written by the Polish Ministry of Foreign Affairs as a plea to the world community to save Polish Jews from the Nazis.

Notes on Bastogne Operation, authored by George S. Patton Jr. shortly after his legendary victory over the Germans in this pivotal battle of the war.

Should Great Britain Go to War--for Czechoslovakia? was written by the Slovak Council in 1937 as "an appeal to British common sense for the sake of World Peace."

Trying to Stop a War in 1939 captures the earnest and
increasingly frantic communications exchanged between
the political and diplomatic representatives of Great
Britain, Poland, Germany and Russia in the year leading
up to the German invasion of Poland in September 1939.
Originally published by the British Foreign Office as a
testament to its extraordinary diplomatic efforts to rein in
Hitler's territorial ambitions, this historically important
collection of speeches, communiqués, cables, letters,
messages and notes has been faithfully reproduced
verbatim.

Polish Literature

Pan Tadeusz, written by Adam Mickiewicz, is a sweeping ode to
Polish history and heritage as seen through the eyes of
two warring families and the lovers caught in the middle.

Amateur Radio

**Quick Study for Your Technician Class Amateur Radio
   License**
Quick Study for Your General Class Amateur Radio License
Quick Study for Your Extra Class Amateur Radio License

Made in the USA
Columbia, SC
09 July 2020